To Ahian from Granny. X

D0246669

SPAM®

THE COOKBOOK

SPAM SPAM

SPAM®

THE COOKBOOK

Marguerite Patten

BB Bounty
Books

First published in 2000 by Hamlyn, an imprint of
Octopus Publishing Group Limited

This edition published in 2007 by Bounty Books, a division of
Octopus Publishing Group Limited, 2–4 Heron Quays,
London E14 4JP
An Hachette Livre UK Company
Reprinted 2007

Project Editor: Sarah Ford
Copy-editor: Anne Crane
Picture researcher: Rosie Garai

Home Economist: Dagmar Vesely

Notes

1 Standard level spoon measurements are used in all recipes.
   1 tablespoon = one 15 ml spoon
   1 tablespoon = one 1¼ American tablespoon
   1 teaspoon = one 5 ml spoon

2 Imperial, metric and American measurements have been given in all recipes.
Use one set of measurements only and not a mixture of both.

3 Measurements for canned food have been given as a standard metric
equivalent.

4 Eggs should be medium unless otherwise stated. The Department of Health
advises that eggs should not be consumed raw. This book contains dishes made
with raw or lightly cooked eggs. It is prudent for more vulnerable people, such as
pregnant and nursing mothers, invalids, the elderly, babies and young children, to
avoid uncooked or lightly cooked dishes made with eggs. Once prepared, these
dishes should be kept refrigerated and used promptly.

5 Milk should be full fat unless otherwise stated.

6 Once a can of SPAM has been opened it can be wrapped and stored in the
refrigerator for 2 days. Leftover SPAM can be frozen.

7 Fresh herbs should be used unless otherwise stated. If unavailable, use dried
herbs as an alternative, but halve the quantities stated.

8 Pepper should be freshly ground black pepper unless otherwise stated.

9 Ovens should be preheated to the specified temperature - if using a fan-
assisted oven, follow the manufacturer's instructions for adjusting the time and
the temperature.

10 This book includes dishes made with nuts and nut derivatives. It is advisable
for customers with known allergic reactions to nuts and nut derivatives and
those who may be potentially vulnerable to these allergies, such as pregnant and
nursing mothers, invalids, the elderly, babies and children, to avoid dishes made
with nuts and nut oils. It is also prudent to check the labels of pre-prepared
ingredients for the possible inclusion of nut derivatives.

Contents

SPAM is a registered trademark for chopped pork and ham owned by Hormel Foods Corporation.

Executive Art Editor: Leigh Jones

Photographer: Sean Myers
Stylist: Clare Hunt

Action Photographer: Anja Koch
Production Controller: Lisa Moore

Introduction

SPAM came to Britain in 1941 as part of the Lend-Lease Agreement with the USA. By 1941 we in Britain had become used to rationing, which began in 1940, but how we longed for tasty food and more variety. SPAM certainly provided a new and welcome change and it was a product that had a distinct and pleasant flavour. I remember so well when I first tasted SPAM. One night every week, after work, I reported for all-night firewatching. A friend was part of the team and we took it in turns to make sandwiches and bring a vacuum flask of tea. On this particular occasion it was my friend who made the sandwiches – and how good they tasted. The bread was spread with the usual microscopic amount of butter (or maybe, margarine) but that did not matter, for the filling was wonderfully moist, not at all dry, and it had a pleasantly spicy taste. It was SPAM.

To many Britons the small amount of meat on the official ration was a real problem. Before the war, most people had enjoyed a generous amount of meat but from 1940 right until 1954 the ration was 1s. 2d. (6p) per person each week. That could be interpreted as two lamb chops, although you could have a larger quantity if you chose cheaper meat. Foods like offal (variety meats) and flavourless, and almost meatless, sausages were not officially rationed and most butchers tried to give all their customers a fair share but supplies were so pitifully small that you would be fortunate if you could get some each week.

You can imagine the enthusiasm that greeted extra meat in the form of canned SPAM. It was a really meaty luncheon meat – each can contained a high percentage of pork so it was a highly nutritious source of protein. Do not imagine you could buy as much SPAM as you liked, however. It was sold under the points scheme. Each civilian was allowed 16 points every month and these points could be used to buy foods such as canned fish or meat, or canned fruit or dried pulses – peas, beans or lentils. Of course, buying the various foods depended upon your grocer receiving adequate supplies. A 340 g/12 oz can of SPAM meant using about eight of those precious points – but it was worth it. SPAM was good solid cooked meat, which could be used straight from the can for salads and sandwiches. It was a splendid basis for a stew, hotpot or pie. Any small amount left could be used in an omelette (generally made with dried eggs during the war years).

One of the most popular dishes of those days, which is still a prime favourite today, was SPAM Fritters. Ask anyone who was at school during the 1940s – and later – about their favourite dish at school dinner and the chances are you will be told that it was SPAM Fritters – crispy batter enclosing tasty slices of SPAM. There is a recipe on page 59 together with interesting suggestions for varying them. If you fancied a traditional Toad-in-the-Hole but the butcher had no sausages, diced SPAM gave the dish a very good flavour.

After the war when supplies of fresh meat, together with poultry and many other foods, became plentiful, SPAM tended to be forgotten by some people but certainly not by everyone. Do you remember those wonderful *Monty Python's Flying Circus* television programmes? SPAM was featured in those: the sketch is described in more detail on pages 34–35.

7

Left: Putting SPAM on a pedestal – the Austin, Minnesota tourism campaign – a giant SPAM can building.

Below: SPAM spans the globe proving to be popular with the Japanese.

Right: The fastest SPAM can in the world, SPAM hits the race track in style.

Far Right: Taste the fun, SPAM fans enjoy one of Hormel's many organized promotional events.

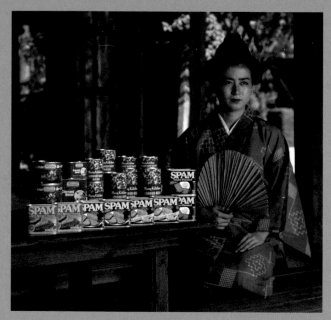

Refrigerators and freezers are not required for its safe preservation. It is a meat that blends with a wide variety of other foods, as illustrated in the recipes that are given in this book. You will enjoy creating your own SPAM dishes, too.

During the war years, civilians in Britain, the USA and other countries and the cooks in the forces served SPAM in simple ways. Nowadays with our taste for dishes from around the world you can use SPAM to make really exciting meals. Whatever kind of food you enjoy cooking and

SPAM has many advantages. You can keep a stock of cans in the storecupboard, where it remains in good condition for a long time.

serving, SPAM enables you to make easy and speedy dishes. Because each can contains such a high percentage of meat you know you and your family are being well fed. As there are neither skin nor bones in the meat even younger children can eat it without any trouble.

SPAM has become so well-known in its homeland, the USA, that a fascinating book *SPAM – A Biography* was written. The cover describes it as The Amazing True Story of America's "Miracle Meat"! I enjoyed reading this book and was grateful to learn many facts about the early days of SPAM. In Britain there is now a **SPAM® FAN CLUB** (see page 57), which has been hailed with great enthusiasm by men, women and children. Members of the club receive newsletters, they can enter competitions and learn of new and exciting ways to serve their favourite luncheon meat. The Club has been most helpful in giving me copies of letters they receive from their enthusiastic members.

In this book I pass on some of my favourite recipes based on SPAM. The ingredients are given in metric, imperial and American measures so everyone can follow them with ease. I hope the facts and recipes in this book will give great pleasure to SPAM lovers and encourage those of you who may not be so familiar with the tasty chopped pork and ham to appreciate what you have been missing.

Marguerite Patten

SPAM®: THE HISTORY

The blend of chopped pork and ham that has become famous under the name of SPAM luncheon meat was created and produced by the Geo. A. Hormel company of Austin, Minnesota, USA. The person responsible for its development was the president of the company, Jay C Hormel, son of the founder George, who had created this large and prosperous company from his modest beginnings as a retail butcher. Jay had shown business acumen from his schooldays and brought many new ideas to the firm. When planning SPAM he envisaged a vastly superior canned luncheon meat based mainly on minced shoulder of prime pork.

At first father George was not impressed with the idea but his son persisted in experiments to achieve a first-class product. He wanted one that was full of flavour, that could be an acceptable alternative to fresh meat, but also would side-step the fluctuating prices and storage problems associated with fresh pork. Jay had already had experience of producing various forms of canned foods, including large cans of ham and spiced ham for butchers and delicatessen shops. The drawback to these was, once opened, the meat had a limited shelf life, even when refrigerated. Traders would slice the amounts required by various customers but had to store the remainder. This made Jay realize that if his new vision of canned meat was to be the success he hoped, the meat had to be canned in small domestic-sized containers.

Various experts on canning were brought in to work on the project. The aim was to produce a firm textured, cooked pork luncheon meat that looked attractive, tasted good and could be served cold from the can or heated in various ways like fresh meat. One of the initial problems was to make sure there was no liquid (loose juice) in the cans.

It is believed that Jean Vernet, the French chef employed by the Hormel company, played a major part in formulating the final flavour of the product.

With all technical difficulties resolved one can imagine everyone's delight when the new product was ready to launch. There was however one problem – **what was it to be called?** Originally it was known as chopped ham but a catchier name was required.

The Christening of SPAM®

This lack of name caused considerable delay before the canned luncheon meat appeared on the market. Various names were suggested but none seemed appropriate. It had to be a brand name that could not be copied by competitors. By late 1936 there was a satisfactory product – ready to be sold – but one without a name.

It is reported that Jay Hormel decided to stage a New Year's party for the express purpose of naming 'his baby'. Guests were to be entitled to a drink for each name they suggested and there would be a prize of $100 for the winner. The host is believed to have commented at a later date that 'by the fourth drink people began to show some imagination'.

The name SPAM was suggested by Kenneth Daigneau, brother of the Hormel vice-president and an actor, who was a guest at the party. He had appeared in various shows on stage and on the radio but certainly was not of star status. However he did choose a wonderfully apt star name for the new luncheon meat and one that was accepted by the firm. SPAM was a short word that everyone would remember; it was easy to pronounce and it described the contents of the can with its combination of **shoulder of pork and ham**.

Above: Jay C Hormel with his many Hormel products.

Right: Kenneth Daigneau who famously gave SPAM a name.

SPAM®'s Launch

SPAM was launched in the USA in May 1937, and began to sell well in spite of the fact that within a short time there were over one hundred competitors. Many of these disappeared in record time, due to their lack of quality. Because SPAM was an inexpensive meat it meant that even poorer families could afford to buy it. By 1938 it had become so popular that it received an award for the best company development of 1937.

Americans were becoming accustomed to television advertising at this time and SPAM commercials were shown on various popular programmes. SPAM featured in the lyric of the first singing TV advertisement to the tune of 'My Bonny Lies over the Ocean'.

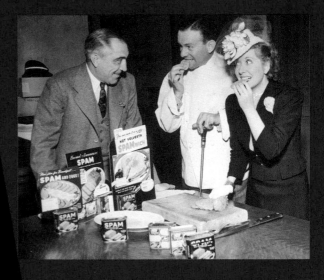

This page and opposite: Early pictures from the Hormel Food Corporation's archives.

Wartime America

In March 1941, Congress passed the Lend-Lease Act which provided aid to the Allied Forces, and many firms, including Hormel, moved into wartime production. SPAM was one of the foods that was sent to Britain for civilians and members of the armed forces. It was also dispatched to the many countries where men and women were serving. When Germany invaded Russia, SPAM helped to feed the hard-pressed people.

Russia's Nikita Kruschev once said 'Without SPAM, we wouldn't have been able to feed our army'.

After Pearl Harbor, the USA joined the Allies and American forces served in many parts of the world; SPAM was needed to feed them. Service personnel are not always complimentary about their food and some GIs formed a less than flattering opinion of SPAM. Obviously the dishes of which it formed a part were often fairly dull, due to the primitive conditions under which they were prepared. Sometimes shortages of alternative foods meant that SPAM was served for breakfast, lunch and dinner on the same day – few people would be delighted at that monotonous menu!

Some complaints may have been caused by the fact that there was a special American Government brand of SPAM, prepared by Hormel, but without the superior flavour of true SPAM. This may well have caused adverse reports about the luncheon meat. You will find some of the comments from GIs and other service personnel on the pages that follow.

Wartime Memories

Irena Urdang de Tour called the packages of SPAM, chocolate and soup she received in the ruins of Warsaw after years of slave labour in Berlin 'ambrosia'.

Some enterprising GIs would trade their cans of SPAM from home for rum or cigarettes. Servicemen from Britain and Canada looked with envy at the generous amounts of food sent to the Americans.

At one period in the United States there was a tin shortage and a ban on the domestic sale of most brand products made by the Hormel firm – except SPAM.

In a letter to Jay Hormel, Mrs Amelia A Garrett of London praised 'the best tinned food that I have tasted in two wars … It's 100 per cent perfect nourishment and tasty'.

Some members of the American forces complained bitterly that they were fed SPAM by the forces' cooks and had cans of SPAM sent from home – as a treat!

SPAM® Fact

Between 1939 and 1942 the sales of SPAM® doubled, and by 1944 90 per cent of all Hormel canned foods were exported to various theatres of war.

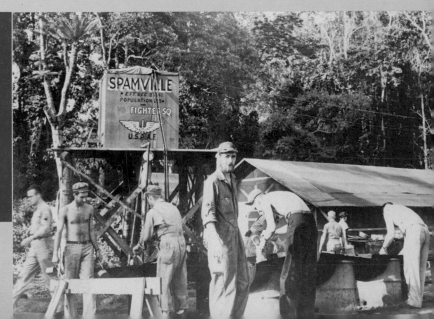

Wartime Britain

The USA's Lend-Lease was a wonderful help to beleaguered Britain. Among the foods we received was concentrated orange juice; this was given to expectant mothers, babies and young children and played an important role in pro-moting good health, for it was a valuable source of vitamin C. Fresh citrus fruits were not available between 1939 and 1945, for all vital shipping space was needed to transport men and military equipment.

In Britain fresh meat was so scarce that from time to time corned beef (often called bully beef) had to form part of the official meat ration. Men and women serving abroad also had corned beef with unwelcome regularity, so both civilians and members of the forces welcomed the new meat by the name of SPAM. Because it came in cans it was easy and safe to transport throughout Britain and to many places further afield.

One of the wartime measures instituted by the British Government was the provision of midday meals for school children. This helped to ensure that growing children had as much nutritious food as was possible in those days. School caterers, like all cooks of the time, had to plan meals with restricted ingredients, so SPAM figured largely in the menus and it proved very popular with the children.

More Wartime Memories

Mr H Ranfield was a prisoner of war in Germany at Stalag Luft 7. The prisoners enjoyed eating SPAM and they also used the cans. They beat these flat with spoons and used them for dispensing trays in the medical rooms.

Mr G Holley served in India during the war. He had beans and corned beef twice a day for much of the time. One day a US Officer appeared with a lorry load of SPAM to exchange for the corned beef. The exchange was a success. The American GIs had corned beef – a change for them – and the British enjoyed the new flavour of SPAM. Mr Holley stills likes SPAM today – but not corned beef.

A meaty subject...

She needs as much meat as he does!

Do heavy workers need more meat?
No. Daily wear and tear on the tissues is not materially affected by the kind of work done.

Mrs E Bowie remembers sitting in an air-raid shelter eating her mother's home-made SPAM sandwiches. She says they went down a treat and even made the family forget about the bombs dropping outside.

Mr T Howard spent his time in the war in the Merchant Navy on a small coaster. They had no refrigeration for fresh meat, so they had SPAM fried for breakfast, cold with salad for lunch and with mashed potatoes for dinner. Modern ships have refrigeration but still serve SPAM.

Madam – important notice!

"SPAM" – is the registered trademark distinguishing the product manufactured exclusively by Geo. A. Hormel & Co., "Spam" is made of pure pork shoulder meat with ham meat added. "Spam" is sold ONLY in 12 oz. tins plainly marked with the trademark "Spam." We are sorry that during the war, supplies of "Spam" are restricted.

"SPAM"
* "Spam" is a registered trademark.

SPAM® Fact

At the end of the war in 1945, SPAM® was sent to help feed the starving people of Europe.

SPAM® – THE RECIPES
All Day Dish

SPAM – chopped pork and ham – is a most versatile meat. It can be sliced, diced or mashed according to the way you would like to serve it. Modern SPAM retains all the fine qualities of the luncheon meat that was first launched in 1937. In addition to classic SPAM there is now SPAMLITE® which has 25 per cent less fat and salt. You can use this or ordinary SPAM in all recipes in the book. The SPAM can of today has changed – no longer is there a key to open it but instead an easy-to-pull ring on the top.

When can you serve SPAM? The answer is whenever you like – SPAM can be enjoyed at any time of the day, from breakfast to a sustaining dinner or a light late-night supper snack.

Breakfast SPAM®: Heat a very little oil in a frying pan. Fry slices of SPAM until piping hot then top with fried eggs. Serve with grilled or fried tomatoes and mushrooms.

Croque Monsieur: Make sandwiches of sliced SPAM and sliced Gruyère or other good cooking cheese. Quickly dip them into beaten egg then fry until crisp and brown on both sides.

SPAM® Rarebit: Top slices of toast with sliced SPAM then cover these with grated or sliced Cheddar, Cheshire or Double Gloucester cheese. Place under a preheated grill (broiler) and heat until the cheese is bubbling and golden brown. To make a more substantial meal, serve the rarebit with grilled or fried tomatoes.

SPAM®
CHOPPED PORK AND HAM

Super Sandwiches

Sandwiches are quick to make, easy to serve and make a nutritious meal to eat at home, at school or work, or to take on a picnic. Today sandwiches can be made more interesting with a choice of modern breads, such as granary, ciabatta or focaccia loaves. SPAM® sandwiches achieved fame during the Second World War. Here are some suggested fillings based on SPAM. The proportion of the various ingredients is a matter of personal choice.

Breakfast Special: Sliced SPAM, scrambled egg, sliced tomatoes and watercress sprigs.

Oriental Treat: Mix mashed SPAM with a little crushed then chopped lemon grass, chopped coriander (cilantro) and a sprinkling of desiccated coconut. Add a very few drops of soy sauce. Top with bean sprouts or bok choy (Chinese leaves).

Full of Crunch: Mix mashed SPAM with finely chopped dessert apple, finely chopped celery and chopped green (bell) pepper.

Hot and Spicy: Mash SPAM with a few drops of Tabasco or chilli sauce or a good pinch of chilli powder, add well-drained and slightly crushed red kidney beans and skinned chopped tomatoes.

Salad Special: Fill the sandwiches with various kinds of lettuce, sliced SPAM, rings of green (bell) pepper, slices of tomato and cucumber.

Sweet and Sour: Drain sweetened canned pineapple rings, then chop them finely, and slice pickled gherkins (sweet dill pickles). Mix the pineapple and gherkins with mashed SPAM. Top with crisp lettuce.

SPAM® for Parties

Here are some interesting party 'nibbles' that can be prepared within minutes.

Crudités with Savoury Dip: To make the crudités, prepare a selection of raw vegetables, e.g. narrow strips of green, yellow and red (bell) pepper, baby carrots, neat pieces of celery and cauliflower florets. To make the dip, put 200 g/7 oz SPAM® into a food processor with 150 ml/¼ pint (⅔ cup) tomato juice and 1 teaspoon Worcestershire sauce and purée until smooth. If preferred, simply mash the SPAM, then gradually add the tomato juice and Worcestershire sauce. Tip the dip into a bowl, stir in 2 tablespoons finely snipped chives, 1 tablespoon finely chopped coriander (cilantro), 1 teaspoon prepared mustard and salt and pepper if required. To serve, spoon the dip into an attractive small bowl and place in the centre of a large platter with the crudités arranged around it.
Serves 4–5

Stuffed Celery: Mash 125 g/4 oz SPAM with 100 g/3½ oz (½ cup) soft cream or curd cheese. Add 1 tablespoon finely chopped nuts. Cut about 20 short lengths of crisp celery and fill the cavities with the SPAM mixture. Top with nuts and/or small pieces of black and green olives.
Makes 20

SPAM®, Apricot and Coconut Balls: Mash 200 g/7 oz SPAM. Cut 50 g/2 oz (⅓ cup) ready-to-eat dried apricots into very small pieces, add to the SPAM and knead well. Form the mixture into small balls. Put 3 tablespoons desiccated coconut on a plate and roll the small balls in this until well coated. Push a cocktail stick through each ball.
Makes 15–18
Variations: Add 1 teaspoon curry paste to the mixture.
• Use prunes instead of apricots.

SPAM® Fact

In Korea, SPAM® is sold in stylish presentation gift boxes with eight cans in each one.

20

Cheese Fondue

This makes an ideal party dish. Squares of SPAM and fresh bread or toast are dipped into the creamy cheese mixture. If you do not possess a proper fondue heater and pot, you can use a heat-resistant bowl placed over a pan of simmering water to melt the cheese. The recipe uses the two classic cheeses but any good cooking cheese, such as Cheddar, can be used. The cornflour is not essential but it helps to prevent the mixture curdling (separating).

Preparation time: 10 minutes
Cooking time: 10–15 minutes
Serves 4

15 g/½ oz (1 tablespoon) butter, softened
1 garlic clove, halved
1 teaspoon cornflour (cornstarch)
300 ml/½ pint (1¼ cups) dry white wine
250 g/8 oz (2 cups) Gruyère cheese, grated
250 g/8 oz (2 cups) Emmenthal cheese, grated
1–2 tablespoons kirsch or brandy (optional)
salt and white pepper
Dippers:
SPAM®, cut into 2.5 cm/1 inch cubes
fresh bread or toast, cut into 2.5 cm/1 inch cubes

Did you know?

SPAM® is sold in 50 countries around the world? For more details, see page 47.

1 Spread or brush the butter around the inside of a ceramic fondue pot (this is more suitable for a cheese fondue than a metal pot, which can become too hot) and then rub with the garlic clove.

2 Blend the cornflour with the wine, and add to the pot with the cheeses. Heat gently over the fondue heater, stirring occasionally.

3 Season to taste with salt and pepper then add the kirsch or brandy, if using. Serve with the dippers, which should be speared on fondue or ordinary forks.

Variations: SPAM® Fondue: Heat cubes of SPAM in hot oil then drain on kitchen paper. Serve dipped in tomato ketchup or mayonnaise. Never try to eat the very hot meat on forks that have been dipped in the oil – they become ultra hot.

21

SPAM® & Mushroom Ramekins

Preparation time: 10 minutes
Cooking time: 12–15 minutes
Serves 4–6

175 g/6 oz (2 cups) button mushrooms, finely chopped
200 g/7 oz SPAM®, finely chopped
2 tablespoons freshly grated Parmesan cheese
1 tablespoon finely chopped parsley
1 egg, beaten
150 ml/5 fl oz single cream (⅔ cup light cream)
1 tablespoon chopped lemon grass (optional)
salt and pepper
flat leaf parsley, to garnish

Grease 4–6 individual ovenproof soufflé dishes. Mix together all the ingredients and spoon into the dishes. Bake in a preheated oven, 200°C/400°F/Gas Mark 6, for 12 minutes or until just firm, then garnish with parsley and serve.

Variations: SPAM® and Egg Ramekins: Omit the mushrooms in the main recipe. Mix together all the ingredients, place in the dishes then break a small egg into each one. Top with a few drops of oil and a sprinkling of Parmesan. Bake as in the main recipe.

• For a softer set egg, bake the SPAM mixture for 5 minutes then add the eggs and topping, return to the oven and continue cooking for a further 7–10 minutes.

Did you know?

That sprinkling a little salt on the board makes it easier to chop or crush garlic.

Savoury Cheesecake

Preparation time: 25 minutes, plus cooling
Cooking time: 1¼ hours
Serves 6–8

Biscuit crust:
75 g/3 oz (⅜ cup) butter, melted
1 teaspoon grated lemon rind
2 teaspoons chopped parsley
175 g/6 oz wholemeal biscuits, crushed (1½ cups Graham crackers, crushed)
salt and pepper

Topping:
500 g/1 lb (2 cups) low-fat curd cheese
250 g/8 oz (1 cup) SPAM®, very finely chopped
1 teaspoon grated lemon rind
2 teaspoons chopped coriander (cilantro)
2 tablespoons finely snipped chives
1 tablespoon chopped parsley
50 g/2 oz (½ cup) carrots, finely grated
25 g/1 oz cornflour (¼ cup cornstarch)
3 large eggs, whisked
2 tablespoons milk or lemon juice

1 Grease a 23–25 cm/9–10 inch springform tin or a cake tin with a loose base. Mix all the ingredients for the biscuit crust and press the mixture into the base of the tin.

2 To make the topping, beat the curd cheese well then gradually add all the other topping ingredients. Season to taste with salt and pepper then spoon the topping over the biscuit crust. Bake in a preheated oven, 150°C/300°F/Gas Mark 2, for about 1¼ hours, or until firm. Leave the cheesecake to cool in the oven with the heat off (to prevent wrinkling). Keep the door of an electric oven ajar, as it will retain heat. When the cheesecake is cold remove it from the tin.

3 The cheesecake can be garnished in various ways, such as dill sprigs, a border of finely chopped SPAM, rings of cooked carrot, radish 'roses', sliced tomatoes or a piped border of cream cheese with small pieces of red and green (bell) peppers and sprigs of parsley and coriander.

SPAM® Porcupine

Cut the SPAM into slices just over 1 cm/½ inch thick, then cut the slices into neat dice. Thread the dice on to cocktail sticks with some of the following ingredients

- baby cocktail onions
- small cocktail gherkins (sweet dill pickles) or diced cucumber
- halved canned pineapple cubes or diced fresh pineapple
- segments of ripe avocado, dipped in lemon juice
- maraschino or glacé cherries.

SPAM is sufficiently firm to allow the sticks to be pushed through the meat without breaking. It is also pleasantly moist and enhances the flavour of the other ingredients. Press the selection of miniature kebabs into a small red or green cabbage or a large grapefruit. The cabbage or grapefruit can be used afterwards.

The cocktail bites can be served with various hot or cold dips, such as

- pesto
- tomato ketchup blended with a little thick yogurt or fromage frais plus a few drops of soy or Worcestershire sauce
- mashed avocado blended with lemon juice and yogurt
- thick tomato purée with a dash of Tabasco sauce or pinch of chilli powder.

SPAM® Fact

If all the cans of SPAM ever eaten were put end-to-end, they would circle the globe at least ten times.

SPAMtastic™ Snacks

Very often one does not require a full meal, but prefers to eat a quick snack instead. On many of these occasions you will find SPAM makes a good choice. It is a wholesome food that provides a generous supply of protein as well as some fat and carbohydrate.

Today, at the start of a new millennium, there are genuine worries that many people, including children, are eating less nutritious foods than they should. Often the household starts the day without any breakfast – why?

There isn't time!

I can't face it.

are just two of the reasons given. On page 18 you will find some easy ideas for breakfast. These do require a short cooking time. If that is a problem, why not adopt the habit that is so popular in Scandinavia and other continental countries and serve a plate of sliced meat (including SPAM) and cheese. This is ready in seconds.

Although it sounds harmless to leave home without eating breakfast, in fact it is not a good thing. It has been shown that physically and mentally we achieve less and often develop a slightly 'sinking' feeling during the middle of the morning. That is when we tend to indulge in sweet snacks which are high in sugar but have very little nutritional value.

Many children and adults take a packed meal to school or work. Sandwiches are a good choice (see page 19 and below), but there are other suggestions given on page 32. These are equally suitable for TV snacks – easy to eat while watching your favourite programmes.

Sandwich Kebabs: Make sandwiches with the fillings given on page 19 but use different breads. Cut the sandwiches into bite-sized pieces and thread on to skewers.

Rolled Sandwiches: Roll thin crustless bread and butter around the fillings.

The Poets Speak

I was intrigued by the flights of fancy produced by various poets to describe, laud or decry SPAM. These are taken from the fascinating American book *SPAM* – *A Biography* by Carolyn Wyman. From Weird Al we have two verses on SPAM and I quote one of these.

If you're running low, go to the store,
Carry some money, to help you buy more,
The tab is there, to open the can,
The can is there, to hold in the SPAM.

The following verse from Moe Tucker is in calypso rhythm.

I'm goin' to work
Little baby, baby
I'm goin' to work
Today.
Mama's going to make
A dollar, dollar
And buy some SPAM
Today.

From less than happy service personnel there were several stanzas – not very complimentary in most cases. I quote my two favourites.

We've had it tucked in salads,
With cabbage for corned beef.
We've had it for an entrée
And also aperitif.
We've had it with spaghetti,
With chili and with rice.
(We all remember one bright day
We had it only twice).

Back home I have an angel
Whose name I want to change.
I'll purchase her a fancy home
With a brand-new modern range;
But marital bliss is sure to cease
If I ever ask for ham
And find my eggs are looking up
For a gol-darned slice of SPAM.

SPAM® Caesar Salad

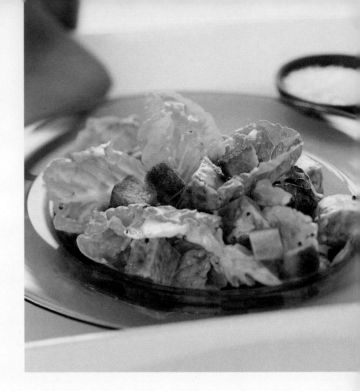

The addition of diced SPAM makes this salad more interesting and sustaining. Plain or garlic croûtons are readily available in supermarkets, but instructions for preparing them are given below. They may be frozen on flat trays, then packed into rigid, freezerproof containers.

Preparation time: 12 minutes
Serves 4

1 garlic clove, halved
1 crisp lettuce, preferably Cos
200 g /7 oz SPAM®, cut into small dice
about 16 plain or garlic croûtons (see below)
Dressing:
1 garlic clove, crushed or chopped
1 teaspoon prepared mustard
2 tablespoons extra virgin olive oil
1–2 teaspoons Worcestershire sauce
1 tablespoon lemon juice
1 tablespoon mayonnaise
3 tablespoons freshly grated Parmesan cheese
salt and pepper

1 Rub the garlic around the sides of a salad bowl. Place the lettuce leaves in the bowl with half the diced SPAM. Mix together all the ingredients for the dressing.

2 Just before serving, toss the lettuce and SPAM in the dressing. Top with the remaining SPAM and the croûtons.

Plain croûtons: Cut 2 slices of crustless bread into 5 mm–1 cm/¼–½ inch dice. Heat 2 tablespoons oil in a frying pan and fry the bread until crisp and golden. Drain on kitchen paper.

Garlic croûtons: Heat 2 tablespoons oil with 2–3 halved garlic cloves for 1 minute. Set aside for 15 minutes for the flavour to develop then proceed as for plain croûtons.

Swedish SPAM®salat

Preparation time: 20 minutes, plus standing
Serves 4–6

2 tablespoons white wine vinegar
1 beetroot, cooked and cut into 2.5cm/1 inch dice
1 large dessert apple, cored but not peeled and cut into
    2.5 cm/1 inch dice
4–5 potatoes, cooked and cut into 2.5 cm/1 inch dice
340 g/12 oz SPAM®, cut into 2.5 cm/1 inch dice
3 tablespoons mayonnaise
2 teaspoons capers
1 tablespoon lemon juice
2 small gherkins (sweet dill pickles), thinly sliced
2 tablespoons chopped spring onions (scallions)
To garnish:
mixed lettuce leaves
chopped dill
2–3 hard-boiled eggs, quartered

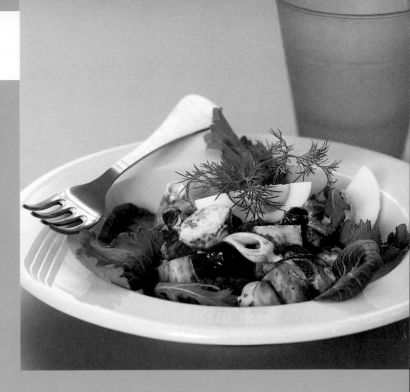

3 To serve, turn out the salad on to a bed of
lettuce, top with the dill and arrange the
quartered eggs around the edge.

1 Pour the vinegar into a large bowl, add the
beetroot and diced apple and leave to stand
for 10 minutes.

2 Add all the remaining ingredients to the
beetroot and apple. Mix well then either
leave in this bowl or transfer to a smaller one.
Cover the salad with a plate and a small weight
and leave in the refrigerator for 1½–2 hours.

SPAM® Fact

You now have the choice of
SPAM® or SPAM LITE®.

29

Tortilla

This Spanish omelette is equally good hot or cold, so it makes a good snack for picnics or part of a packed meal. As it is not folded but served flat, use an 18–20 cm/7–8 inch omelette or frying pan.

Preparation time: 15 minutes
Cooking time: 13 minutes
Serves 2

1 tablespoon olive oil
1 small onion, finely chopped
1 potato, cooked and cut into 5 mm/¼ inch dice
125 g/4 oz SPAM®, cut into 5 mm/¼ inch dice
4 large eggs, beaten
25 g/1 oz (2 tablespoons) butter
1 tablespoon chopped parsley
salt and pepper
snipped chives, to garnish

Cooking Tip

Tortilla and other omelettes can be cooked in suitable dishes in the microwave.

1 Heat the oil in a 18–20 cm/7–8 inch pan, add the onion and cook for 5 minutes. Add the potato and SPAM, cook for 3 minutes then tip into the bowl with the beaten eggs. Season with salt and pepper and mix well.

2 Heat the butter in the pan, add the egg mixture and parsley and cook until the tortilla is firm. Slide it on to a plate, cut into wedges and garnish with snipped chives.

Variations: Instead of cooking the onion, heat thinly sliced spring onions (scallions) with the potato and SPAM. These add a touch of crispness to the tortilla.
• **Pepper Tortilla:** Add a little chopped raw or cooked red and/or green (bell) pepper and/or cooked peas to the potato and SPAM.
• **SPAM® Omelette:** Add 50 g/2 oz (¼ cup) finely diced SPAM for every 2 eggs. Cook in the usual way. Chopped coriander (cilantro) adds colour and flavour.

Bread and SPAM®

We are fortunate nowadays that good bakers and supermarkets sell a wide range of continental breads. Several of these offer a great variety for making interesting snacks.

FROM FRANCE
Baguette Sandwiches: Split short French loaves (baguettes) lengthways. Spread the cut surfaces with a very little butter (this can be flavoured with Dijon mustard). Sandwich the two halves together with sliced SPAM, chopped black olives, crisp lettuce and sliced tomatoes. Cut into thick segments to serve.
• The SPAM® Pâté on page 43 may be spread on the bread instead of butter.

FROM ITALY
SPAM® and Pepper Bruschetta: Halve and deseed red, green and yellow (bell) peppers. Place under a preheated grill (broiler) with the rounded sides uppermost and heat until the skins blacken. Put into a polythene bag until cold then strip away the skins and cut the peppers into segments. Place the segments on a piece of foil on the grill pan, brush with a little oil and heat for several minutes then set aside. Toast 6 slices of ciabatta bread, rub with a cut garlic clove and moisten with olive oil. Top the bread with slices

of SPAM then with the cooked peppers. Heat for 2–3 minutes then serve.

SPAM® Crostini: Prepare the 6 slices of ciabatta bread (see bruschetta left). Mash 200 g/7 oz SPAM, mix with 2 tablespoons chopped sun-dried tomatoes, 2 tablespoons chopped green olives and spread on the toast. Top with a generous layer of freshly grated Parmesan cheese then brown under the grill (broiler).

FROM GREECE
Savoury Pitta Breads: Dice some SPAM, mix with a little mayonnaise then add some pine nuts, a good pinch of ground cumin and a pinch of ground cinnamon. Fill the pockets in pitta breads with lettuce, sliced tomatoes and a little feta cheese then top with the SPAM mixture.

SPA
CHOPPED PORK AND HAM

Children in the Kitchen

Many children enjoy helping in the kitchen and creating special dishes. Children with poor and finicky appetites may well be inclined to eat better if they have assisted in preparing the dish. A number of the recipes on the previous pages are very easy for children to make and so are SPAMBURGER™s – a favourite snack – which follows on this page. SPAMBURGER™s are perfect for their school lunchboxes – or to serve at any time. They can be made suitable for lunch or dinner if served with an interesting salad or vegetables rather than in a burger bun.

Obviously younger children should not attempt to open cans of food or slice or chop ingredients without an older person being on hand to help them. Neither should they deal with very hot pans of food.

SPAMBURGER™s

Split soft burger rolls or baps and fill them with crisp lettuce, tomato slices, then thick slices of SPAM and slices of cheese. Rings of mild (red) onion and tomato ketchup may be added, or use a small amount of a favourite chutney.

Variations: Hot SPAMBURGER™s: Grill or fry the slices of SPAM then add to the other ingredients and serve at once.

• **Crunchy SPAMBURGER™s:** Mash SPAM and mix with finely chopped red and/or green (bell) pepper, sliced spring onions (scallions) and a very little fresh tomato pulp or tomato ketchup. Form into rounds or squares and serve.

• **Fruity SPAMBURGER™s:** Omit the cheese, add rings of fresh or well-drained canned pineapple or dessert apple rings (dipped in lemon juice to keep them a good colour).

• **Nutty SPAMBURGER™s:** Spread the split buns with peanut butter and add chopped nuts to mashed SPAM, then shape and put into the burger buns. Make sure no one is allergic to nuts.

Monty Python and SPAM®

Monty Python Flying Circus was an exceptionally popular television series in the 1970s. The humour was so clever and unusual; of all the sketches, the one which highlighted SPAM was one of the most memorable. To remind older readers of the episode, and to introduce younger ones, I give a brief extract from that December programme.

Imagine a café where for some unknown reason the rest of the customers seated were Vikings.

Enter Mr and Mrs Bun – not by the door – but flying on wires. They sit down at a table.

Mr. Bun Morning.

Waitress Morning.

Mr. Bun What have you got then?

Waitress Well, there's egg and bacon; egg, sausage and bacon; egg and Spam; egg, bacon and Spam; egg, bacon, sausage and Spam; Spam, bacon, sausage and Spam; Spam, egg, Spam, Spam, bacon and Spam; Spam, Spam; egg and Spam; Spam, Spam, Spam; Spam, Spam, Spam, baked beans, Spam, Spam, Spam and Spam; or a lobster thermidor aux crevettes with a Mornay sauce garnished with truffle pâté, brandy and a fried egg on top and Spam.

Mrs. Bun Have you got anything without Spam in it?

Waitress Well, Spam, egg, sausage and Spam. That's not got much Spam in it.

Mrs. Bun I don't want any Spam.

Mr. Bun Why can't she have egg, bacon, Spam and sausage?

Mrs. Bun That's got Spam in it!

Mr. Bun Not as much as Spam, egg, sausage and Spam.

Mrs. Bun Look, could I have egg, bacon, Spam and sausage without the Spam?

Waitress Uuuuuuuuuuugggh!

Mrs. Bun What d'you mean, uuugggh? I don't like Spam!

Vikings (singing) Spam, Spam, Spam, Spam.

Spam, Spam, Spam, Spam. Lovely Spam, wonderful Spam.
(Brief stock shot of a Viking Ship)
Lovely Spam, wonderful Spam ...
Waitress Shut up! Shut up! Shut up! You can't have egg, bacon, Spam and sausage without the Spam.

The sketch continues with the waitress and the Buns becoming more and more hysterical and concludes with the Vikings singing the SPAM song, a visit by a **Hungarian,** then a visit by a **policeman** and then a **Historian** who announces that the Vikings had won another great victory and explains their military strategy in pompous detail, using a map with arrows on it. Within a few minutes, he too is infected by the atmosphere of the café and can say nothing but Spam, Spam, Spam, Spam ...

At the time of the programme it reminded the British of the SPAM they liked so much (or so little in some cases). What an outstanding advertisement for a product!

SPAM® for Lunch

Busy people will find SPAM an ideal food on which to base lunch dishes. This section starts with suggestions for eating out of doors, at a picnic or a barbecue, for most of us want to make the most of warm sunny days. It continues with several appetizing dishes that are suitable for the middle of the day.

The SPAM Pâté on page 43 is an excellent hors d'oeuvre but it is equally good as a light main course, served with crusty rolls or bread and a salad. When globe artichokes are in season they can be served with this pâté instead of butter, or an oil and vinegar dressing. Scoop out the centre choke of the hot or cold artichoke and fill the hole with SPAM Pâté. Try filling raw or cooked small mushrooms or firm ripe tomatoes with the pâté. As you need to scoop out the centre pulp from the tomatoes, this could be added to a salad dressing. When you put this pâté with hot foods it melts sufficiently to make a thick flavoursome sauce. There are two very good salads on this page but you can use SPAM, and your imagination, to create many more.

Apple and Beetroot Salad: Dice equal quantities of cooked skinned beetroot, unpeeled dessert apples and SPAM, and mix together. Moisten with a dressing made with equal quantities of yogurt and mayonnaise and flavoured with freshly chopped mint and parsley and a dash of lemon juice. Serve on a bed of rocket and/or watercress.

Over the years we have experimented with many more mixtures of foods. Once upon a time people felt that meat and fish should never be combined as one dish – now we know better. This mixture of prawns and SPAM is very good.

Prawn and SPAM® Salad: Neatly dice 340 g/ 12 oz SPAM, mix it with 175 g/6 oz peeled prawns (1 cup shelled shrimp), 2 skinned and diced tomatoes and 4 tablespoons finely diced cucumber. Moisten with mayonnaise flavoured with chopped dill or fennel leaves and a little white wine or white wine vinegar. Serve on a bed of crisp lettuce and garnish with wedges of lime or lemon.

Making Kebabs

SPAM is an ideal meat to use for kebabs, as it is sufficiently firm not to crumble when threaded on to skewers.

SPAM' Kebabs: Cut SPAM into 4–5 cm/ 1½–2 inch dice. Thread on long metal skewers with cherry (very small) tomatoes, portions of green, red and yellow (bell) peppers and small mushrooms. Brush with a little oil or Barbecue Sauce and cook over the barbecue. Turn once or twice, basting with more oil or sauce. Use tongs – never your hands – to turn the skewers. Take the food off the very hot skewers to eat it.

Barbecue Sauce: Finely chop 1 onion and 2 garlic cloves. Heat 2 tablespoons sunflower oil in a saucepan, add the onion and cook for a few minutes, then add the garlic with 2 tablespoons brown or red wine vinegar, 2 tablespoons tomato ketchup, 1 tablespoon brown sugar, 1–2 teaspoons soy sauce and 1–2 teaspoons Worcestershire sauce. Heat well then add about 5 tablespoons chicken stock to give the right consistency. Season to taste with salt and pepper. This amount of sauce serves 4–6.

SPAM' Satay: While you can use metal skewers for this dish the meat is generally placed on bamboo sticks (quite easy to obtain from Oriental stores and large supermarkets). New bamboo sticks should be soaked in very hot water before using; this prevents them burning over the barbecue. Satay sauce traditionally contains peanuts so make sure none of your guests is allergic to peanuts, before you serve it.

   First make the marinade. Finely chop 1 onion and crush 2 garlic cloves. Add 2 teaspoons crushed and chopped lemon grass or lemon zest, 1 tablespoon sunflower oil, 2 teaspoons soy sauce, a little chopped coriander (cilantro) and a pinch of chilli powder or 1 small chopped red chilli. Cut about 750 g/1½ lb SPAM into 2.5 cm/ 1 inch dice and leave in the marinade for 1 hour. Drain and put on to the sticks. Heat well then serve with Satay Sauce.
This dish serves 6–8.

Satay Sauce: Purée 3 tablespoons peanut butter with 150 g/5 oz (¾ cup) peanuts (preferably roasted), 150 ml/¼ pint (⅔ cup) coconut milk, 1 tablespoon lime juice, 1 tablespoon brown sugar, 2 teaspoons soy sauce, a little grated root ginger if desired and salt and pepper to taste. Serve hot or cold.

SPAM® & Pepper Quiche

Preparation time: 30 minutes, plus chilling
Cooking time: 55 minutes
Serves 6–8

Shortcrust pastry (basic pie dough):
125 g/4 oz butter
250 g/8 oz plain flour (2 cups plain all-purpose flour), sifted
water, to mix
Filling:
1 red (bell) pepper, halved and deseeded
1 green (bell) pepper, halved and deseeded
1 yellow (bell) pepper, halved and deseeded
200 g/7 oz SPAM®, finely diced
175 g/6 oz (1½ cups) Gruyère or Cheddar cheese, grated
3 large eggs or 2 large eggs and 2 egg yolks
250 ml/8 fl oz (1 cup) milk
150 ml/¼ pint single cream (⅔ cup light cream) or extra milk
salt and pepper

1 To make the pastry, rub the fat into the flour until the mixture resembles breadcrumbs. Stir in enough water to make a firm dough. Knead lightly and chill for 30 minutes.

2 Heat a baking sheet in the oven as this helps to crisp the base of the quiche. Roll out the pastry and line a 23–25 cm/9–10 inch flan tin or dish, at least 2.5 cm/1 inch deep. To keep the pastry a good shape fill the pastry case with foil or greaseproof paper and baking beans. Put the flan tin on the heated baking sheet and bake blind (empty) in a preheated oven, 200°C/400°F/ Gas Mark 6, for nearly 15 minutes.

3 Meanwhile, heat the peppers under the grill (broiler) until the skins blacken. Put them into a polythene bag. When they are cold, strip away the skins and chop the pulp finely. Lower the oven heat to 160°C/325°F/Gas Mark 3.

4 Remove the baking beans and foil or paper from the pastry case. Spoon in the SPAM, cheese and peppers. Beat the eggs, or eggs and yolks, with the milk and cream and salt and pepper. Carefully pour or strain over the filling. Bake for 40 minutes or until set. Serve hot or cold.

38

Deep SPAM® Pizza

Preparation time: 20 minutes
Cooking time: 30–35 minutes
Serves 1–2

25 cm/10 inch ready-made pizza base
200 g/7 oz SPAM®, thinly sliced
100 g/3½ oz mozzarella cheese, thinly sliced
2 teaspoons chopped oregano
a few black olives (optional)
2 tablespoons freshly grated Parmesan cheese
Tomato layer:
1 tablespoon olive oil
1 onion, finely sliced
2 garlic cloves, finely chopped
250 g/8 oz (1 cup) canned chopped tomatoes
1 tablespoon tomato purée (tomato paste)
salt and pepper

1 First make the tomato layer. Heat half the oil in a pan, add the onion and cook for 5 minutes. Add the garlic, tomatoes, tomato purée and a little salt and pepper and simmer until it becomes a thick purée.

2 Place the pizza base on a preheated baking sheet, brush the inside with the remaining oil and spread the tomato mixture evenly over the base. Top with the SPAM, sliced mozzarella, oregano, olives and finally the grated Parmesan. Place in a preheated oven, 220°C/425°F/Gas Mark 7, and bake for 15–20 minutes or until piping hot.

Variations: Include a layer of sliced raw or cooked mushrooms, cooked aubergine (eggplant) or courgette (zucchini) or red and/or green (bell) pepper slices with the SPAM.
• Instead of preparing a tomato layer, use about 4 tablespoons herb-flavoured tomato pasta sauce or top the pizza base with thinly sliced tomatoes, chopped spring onions (scallions) and/or chives and a little olive oil then with the SPAM and other ingredients.

SPAM® Fact
The ladies who were engaged to promote SPAM® in song were known as SPAMETTES.

39

SPAM® Slippers

Preparation time:
25 minutes, plus standing
Cooking time: 35 minutes
Serves 4

2 large aubergines (eggplants)
½ tablespoon olive oil
salt and pepper
Filling:
2 tablespoons olive oil
2 onions, finely chopped
2 garlic cloves, finely chopped
2 large tomatoes, skinned and chopped
340 g/12 oz SPAM®
1 teaspoon paprika
1 tablespoon chopped coriander (cilantro)
Topping:
4 tablespoons soft breadcrumbs
4 tablespoons grated Gruyère or Cheddar cheese
To garnish:
tomato slices
coriander (cilantro) sprigs

Did you know?

Stuffed aubergines are often known as 'slippers' because of their shape.

1 Halve the aubergines lengthways then run a knife around the edges about 5 mm/¼ inch from the skins. Sprinkle with salt and leave for 30 minutes. Drain away the liquid, rinse in cold water and dry well. Brush the cut surfaces with the ½ tablespoon olive oil.

2 Put the aubergines into a dish, cover with foil and bake in a preheated oven, 200°C/400°F/Gas Mark 6, for 20 minutes. Scoop out the soft centre part of the aubergines and mash it.

3 Meanwhile, heat the 2 tablespoons oil in a saucepan, add the onions and cook for 5 minutes. Add the garlic and tomatoes and cook for a further 10 minutes. Finely chop three-quarters of the SPAM and add it to the saucepan with the paprika, coriander, aubergine pulp and salt and pepper to taste. Spoon the filling into the aubergine shells and top with the bread-crumbs and cheese. Return to the oven for 15 minutes, then serve garnished with the tomato slices, strips of the remaining SPAM and coriander sprigs.

SPA

Here's Progress

In SPAM: The History, which begins on page 10, the story of SPAM after the Second World War is described in brief. However, it is interesting to examine in more detail just how the luncheon meat fared for the rest of the 20th century. By the 1950s, SPAM had won rapid renown in the USA and Britain and various other countries during the years of crisis.

The start of the 1950s was still a worrying period, so many countries were suffering from the aftermath of war, refugees need help to return to their home countries and there were food shortages to be overcome. Britain endured strict rationing up to the end of 1954. SPAM therefore was still a standby for many people, so its sales were high. The surprising thing however was the incredible volume of these sales. The question many people asked was: **'Will this popularity continue, or will it end?'**

In 1959 it was recorded that the **one billionth** can of SPAM was sold, after just 22 years on the market. Since then checks have been kept on its sales worldwide. In 1970 the sales of SPAM reached the **second billion.** In 1980 the **third billion.** In 1986 the **fourth billion.** In 1994 the **fifth billion.** There is the answer **as to whether its popularity endures – SPAM enjoys ever-increasing sales.**

Whenever there are events commemorating the Second World War you can be sure there are displays of SPAM, both in the USA and at the Imperial War Museum in London.

At the present time it is recorded that among 60 million Americans consume SPAM at the rate of 3.6 cans a second. This is the equivalent to 216 cans per minute or 12,960 cans per hour.

In Britain, Tulip International, who distribute SPAM from their parent company in Denmark, find they have achieved record sales. Tulip International have a very fine reputation for all their meat products: that is why they were awarded the licence to produce SPAM by Hormel Foods.

In December 1999 a review of the 20th century's top brand-name products in Britain was produced. Fifty names were listed: these covered alcohol, confectionery, dairy products, household items and groceries, and included the best-known brands of bread, sugar, tea and coffee, together with toiletries.

Within that list was SPAM – a positive proof that we in Britain echo the esteem with which the canned luncheon meat is held in so many parts of the world.

Tulip International report that sales of SPAM are growing by 30 per cent, year by year.

Eating Out of Doors

In these days of insulated boxes and bags, picnics can be grand occasions, where a variety of foods may be served at the planned destination with great elegance, or they can be very simple. One of the easiest picnic menus is SPAM with fresh bread or rolls, a selection of simple salad ingredients and fresh fruit. There is no need to take a can-opener, simply pull the ring at the top of the can of meat and there it is – appetizing pork ready to serve.

For somewhat more elaborate picnics, look at the dishes on pages 23–31or make SPAMburgers (see page 33) or sandwiches, such as those on page 19. Always remember to take something to drink with your picnic, the fresh air makes you thirsty as well as hungry.

Over the years barbecues have become much less expensive – although there are plenty of luxury models available. This method of outdoor cooking and serving food is extremely popular with both adults and children. It is important that there is plenty of supervision if children are around, for barbecues can become dangerously hot. For successful results, the barbecue must be adequately heated before food is placed over it.

One of the simplest and most popular dishes is **Stuffed Jacket Potatoes.** Prick large well-scrubbed potatoes with a fork, cook over the barbecue (or in the oven or microwave, if this is more convenient), halve or take a slice off the top. Scoop out the potato pulp, mash it with butter or margarine and season well with salt and pepper. Spoon the filling back into the potato skins, making good centre cavities. Fill the cavities with diced SPAM in a cheese, mushroom, pesto, or tomato sauce or Barbecue Sauce (see page 37). Put the potatoes back over the barbecue for a few minutes until they are piping hot. Serve on plates or thick pieces of foil.

Barbecued SPAM: Cut really thick slices of SPAM, brush each side with a little oil or oil and orange juice and heat over the barbecue. Just before serving top with brown sugar or honey on the top side. There is no need to turn these slices during cooking. Serve with barbecued mushrooms, tomatoes and salad. You can brush the slices with Barbecue Sauce (see page 37), before and during cooking.

SPAM®

ED PORK AND HAM

SPAM® Pâté

Preparation time: 15 minutes, plus chilling
Serves 4–6

340 g/12 oz SPAM®
50 g/2 oz (¼ cup) butter, melted
2 teaspoons Dijon mustard
2 tablespoons chopped parsley
2 teaspoons chopped basil
6 small gherkins (sweet dill pickles), thinly sliced
2 tablespoons chopped sun-dried tomatoes
6 black olives, pitted and diced
a little sherry, to moisten
salt and pepper
To serve:
toast
cranberry sauce

1   Mash the SPAM in a bowl, add the hot butter and the mustard and mix very well.

2   Stir in the remainder of the ingredients but take care not to break up the diced ingredients, for these add colour and interest to the pâté. Add just enough sherry to moisten the mixture; do not make it too wet – about 1 tablespoon should be sufficient.

3   Spoon into a dish, cover and chill overnight or for several hours. Turn out and serve with toast and cranberry sauce.

Variations: Use double (heavy) cream instead of sherry to give a creamier taste.
• A few raw or lightly cooked and chopped mushrooms can also be added to the mixture.
• A few skinned pistachio nuts add colour and texture to any pâté.

Did you know?

SPAM® first came on to the market in 1937. See page 12.

43

Time for Tea

Teatime has been an important feature of the British lifestyle since the 1840s. It is believed that the Duchess of Bedford of that era created the afternoon meal to fill the gap between luncheon and dinner. During recent years, elaborate teas in private homes have almost vanished during the week, but however rushed you may be on weekdays, it is worthwhile planning an appetizing tea at the weekend. All the preparations can be made in advance so that the cook, as well as everyone else, can sit back and enjoy a leisurely meal.

Afternoon tea has become the fashion once more in a number of smart hotels. The meal is enjoyed so much that in London, and other large towns and cities, it is advisable to book a table in advance to make sure of being served.

A true afternoon tea menu reflects the traditions of the past. It should include small savoury sandwiches (with the crusts cut off, of course); the suggestions on page 19 for interesting sandwich fillings are ideal. There may be plates of wafer-thin bread and butter, and scones (biscuits) served with preserves and often with clotted or whipped cream, followed by a selection of cakes and biscuits (cookies). A choice of teas, such as China, Earl Grey and Indian, will be offered.

A different kind of teatime meal is still served in many homes, particularly those in the north of England and in Scotland. It is known as high tea and it is very practical where there are younger children. The children get a sustaining meal after coming home from school and well before going to bed. With this kind of tea there is always a savoury dish, often cold meat such as SPAM, with salad, plenty of bread and butter, tea and cakes. Nowadays modern savouries, such as a pizza (see page 39) or quiche (see page 38) will be a regular part of the meal and the cakes replaced with fruit of some kind, and maybe a savoury cheesecake (see page 23).

SPA

Whether your teatime is long and leisurely, or just consists of a quick cup of tea, do make the SPAM Scones on the opposite page. They are delicious and freeze well, so you can make a large batch. We are urged to cut down on sweet dishes and replace these with savoury ones. These scones go just as well with coffee as with tea. They will be a popular extra for a packed meal or to take on a picnic.

SPAM® Scones

Preparation time: 10 minutes
Cooking time: 12–15 minutes
Makes 10–12

250 g/8 oz (2 cups) self-raising flour, or plain (all-purpose) flour
    with 2 teaspoons baking powder
pinch of salt
25 g/1 oz (2 tablespoons) butter or margarine
150 g/5 oz (nearly ⅜ cup) SPAM®, cut into 3 mm/⅛ inch dice
about 150 ml/¼ pint (⅔ cup) milk, plus extra for glazing
Filling:
butter or margarine
SPAM®
segments of tomato and cucumber

1 Lightly grease a baking sheet or line it with baking parchment. Sift together the flour, or flour and baking powder, and salt in a bowl. Rub in the butter or margarine, add the SPAM and enough milk to make a soft rolling consistency.

2 Roll out the dough on a lightly floured board to 1.5 cm/¾ inch thick. Cut it into small rounds and brush the tops with the milk. Place the rounds on the baking sheet and bake in a preheated oven, 220°C/425°F/Gas Mark 7, for 12–15 minutes until the scones feel firm when pressed at the sides.

3 Serve the scones hot with butter. Alternatively, leave them to cool, then split and spread with a little butter, slices of SPAM and tomato and cucumber.

Variation: Vegetable Cobbler: Roast a mixture of vegetables, or make a vegetable casserole. When it is nearly cooked place the scones on top of the hot vegetables and bake as above.

Did you know?

SPAM® cans were used during the war to make dispensing trays. See page 17.

SPAM® for Dinner

Dinner is the most important meal in most households, whether it is eaten at night or in the middle of the day. Nowadays we enjoy a wide range of dishes, including some based on pasta and rice, influenced by the cooking styles of other countries. The dishes selected here should please most people, they are very varied. If you like Oriental stir-frys, turn to page 53 for **Pork & Fruit Stir-fry**, while if you like seafood and rice, there is a wonderful medley of ingredients in the **Penny-wise Paella** on page 50.

One recipe, of the utmost historical importance, is the one for **SPAM® Fritters** on page 59. Undoubtedly this was the most popular dish with young and old in Britain during the Second World War. The liking for fritters of all kinds goes back to ancient Greek and Roman times; that is why I have devoted page 58 to the history of these fried delicacies.

Good cooking takes time and trouble, but most of the dishes in this book can be prepared and cooked within a short time, which is in keeping with our busy modern lifestyle. Some people have very little time to cook and very little space to store equipment and prepare and cook their meals. I refer to those, both young and old, who live in very simple accommodation – possibly on campus or in lodgings while at college or university, or in a small retirement home. There are special ideas to make cooking really easy, starting on page 56.

It is important, however restricted your cooking facilities, to have well-planned and nourishing meals. Eating at home is much cheaper than going to even modest restaurants. SPAM is an inexpensive meat, and provides nutritious protein food at a low cost. Fortunately there are no problems with storage. You can keep the cans in your storecupboard since until it is opened the meat is safe for up to five years.

SPAM® Around the World

SPAM was first launched in 1937 at Austin, Minnesota, USA. For several years after that date it was sold successfully throughout the United States but nowhere else. In 1942 the situation changed with great suddenness. SPAM was sent to Britain to help eke out the limited wartime rations. In addition it went to many spheres of war where the Allied Forces were serving – thus SPAM became known in many very different countries.

When the Second World War ended in 1945 it was apparent that many people in the world were starving so SPAM, with other products, was sent to aid the hungry. Their appreciation was clearly expressed and undoubtedly led to a desire to continue to enjoy what is sometimes known as 'the miracle meat'.

Many American service personnel had been fed SPAM so often that they were less than complimentary. Some vowed never to eat SPAM again when they returned home. Maybe in time they changed their minds and bought SPAM.

As the years passed SPAM reached many more countries. Now the meat is eaten from Alaska to Australia – and from Japan and Korea in the Far East to Canada – and each country gives a special taste to their SPAM dishes. In fact SPAM is sold in 50 countries throughout the world and trade-

marked in 100. It is not sold in Islamic countries for their inhabitants do not eat pork.

SPAM looks the same all round the world, except in Canada and Australia. In Canada the label on cans of SPAM LITE reads SPAM Léger, in deference to the French Canadians, and in Australia it is described as SPAM Spiced Ham instead of Chopped Pork and Ham. However, it tastes just as good all round the world.

47

SPAM

Neapolitan SPAM® & Penne

Preparation time: 15 minutes
Cooking time: 20 minutes
Serves 4

2 tablespoons olive oil
1 onion, finely chopped
2 garlic cloves, finely chopped
400 g/13 oz (scant 2 cups) canned chopped plum tomatoes
1 tablespoon tomato purée (tomato paste)
100 g/3½ oz (generous cup) small button mushrooms
340 g/12 oz SPAM®, cut into narrow fingers
1 tablespoon chopped basil
250 g/8 oz penne
salt and pepper
To garnish:
freshly shredded Parmesan cheese
basil leaves
a few capers (optional)

1   Heat the oil in a large saucepan, add the
onion and cook for 5 minutes then add the
garlic and cook for a further 2 minutes. Add the
tomatoes and stir in the tomato purée and
mushrooms. Cook for 5 minutes, stirring once or
twice, then add the SPAM, basil and salt and
pepper to taste. Cook gently for 5–6 minutes.

2   Meanwhile, cook the penne in boiling salted
water until tender. Strain and put on to a
hot dish. Top with the SPAM mixture then the
Parmesan, basil and capers, if using.

Variation: Use other pasta shapes such as
conchiglie (shells) or farfalle (butterflies). If using
longer strands of pasta dice the SPAM finely.

Cooking Pasta

Always allow at least
1.2 litres/2 pints (5 cups)
of liquid to each 125 g/4 oz
of pasta.

Rice and SPAM®

SPAM adds interest and food value to a number of rice dishes. To turn plain cooked rice into a satisfying dish add chopped herbs, such as parsley, sage and basil, diced SPAM and a few skinned chopped tomatoes. Heat with the rice then serve at once.

The following are more classic dishes.

Mushroom and SPAM® Risotto: Use risotto (arborio) rice to produce the correct creamy texture. Buy about 250 g/8 oz mushrooms. You can choose all cultivated mushrooms or all wild ones. A mixture of chestnut, shiitake and oyster mushrooms imparts an interesting appearance and texture. Finely chop 1 onion, wipe the mushrooms, or rinse them in cold water, and slice thickly. Heat 25 g/1 oz (2 tablespoons) butter and 1 tablespoon olive oil in a large saucepan. Add the onion and cook gently for 5 minutes. Stir in 250 g/8 oz (1 cup plus 2 tablespoons) rice, making sure every grain is coated with fat. Meanwhile, in another saucepan, heat 900 ml/1½ pints (3¾ cups) well-seasoned chicken stock plus a good pinch of saffron threads or powdered saffron. Add about one-third of this hot liquid to the rice with the mushrooms. Stir and cook steadily until all the liquid is absorbed. Continue like this, adding liquid to the rice until the rice is nearly tender. Stir in 250 g/8 oz neatly diced SPAM and 25 g/1 oz (2 tablespoons) butter and any extra salt and pepper required. Heat well and serve topped with freshly grated Parmesan cheese.
Serves 4

Spicy SPAM® Pilau: Finely chop 2 onions and 2 garlic cloves. Heat 2 tablespoons olive oil in a large saucepan. Add the onions and cook steadily for 5 minutes. Stir in the garlic with ½ teaspoon ground coriander and generous pinches of cumin, chilli powder, cinnamon and turmeric plus a shake of cayenne pepper. Heat gently for 2 minutes, then stir in 250 g/8 oz (1 cup plus 2 tablespoons) long-grain white or brown rice plus 750 ml/ 1¼ pints (scant 3 cups) chicken stock or water, 3 tablespoons raisins and 3 tablespoons pine nuts. Simmer steadily until the rice is almost cooked then stir in 340 g/12 oz neatly diced SPAM and heat thoroughly.
Serves 4–6
Variation: Add a little lemon juice and 2–3 skinned chopped tomatoes to the pilau to enhance the flavour.

Penny-wise Paella

This interesting mixture of meat and fish is one of Spain's outstanding recipes. The cooked dish should be pleasantly moist so a generous amount of stock is required.

Preparation time: 30 minutes
Cooking time: 35 minutes
Serves 4–6

2 tablespoons olive oil
2 onions, finely chopped
2 garlic cloves, finely chopped
250 g/8 oz (1 cup plus 2 tablespoons) long-grain rice
900 ml/1½ pints (3¾ cups) chicken stock
½ teaspoon saffron threads or powdered saffron
3 tomatoes, skinned and chopped
1 red (bell) pepper, cored, deseeded and diced
340 g/12 oz SPAM®, cut into narrow fingers
250 g/8 oz (1½ cups) cooked peas
about 18 mussels, cooked and on single shells
about 12 large prawns, cooked and peeled (shrimp, shelled)
salt and pepper

1 Heat the oil in a very large frying pan or a paella pan – if you have one. Add the onion and cook for 5 minutes.

2 Add the garlic and cook for 2 minutes then stir in the rice and continue stirring until each grain is coated with oil.

3 Pour in the chicken stock, then stir in the saffron, tomatoes, red pepper and salt and pepper to taste. Cook steadily until the rice is almost tender then add the SPAM and cooked peas. Stir to blend the ingredients and cook for a further 5 minutes. If the mixture is a little too moist cook fairly vigorously for a few minutes so the excess liquid evaporates.

4 Finally add the shellfish and heat for just a few minutes then serve.

Did you know?

Saffron comes from a special crocus and is the most expensive spice in the world.

50

Chicken Cordon Bleu

SPAM's rich flavour makes it an ideal ingredient to use in stuffings for other meats, chicken and vegetables. In this version of a classic dish it helps to keep lean chicken breasts beautifully moist.

Preparation time: 20 minutes
Cooking time: 15–18 minutes
Serves 4

4 boneless chicken breasts
1 tablespoon flour
1 egg, beaten
about 50 g/2 oz (½ cup) soft breadcrumbs
50 g/2 oz (¼ cup) butter
2 tablespoons sunflower oil
salt and pepper
mixed vegetables, to serve
Filling:
150 g/5 oz SPAM®, mashed
4 tablespoons grated Gruyère or Cheddar cheese
1 tablespoon single (light) cream
1 teaspoon chopped rosemary
1 tablespoon chopped parsley

1 First make the filling. Mix the SPAM with the other filling ingredients. Form the mixture into a neat shape and cut it into 4 equal portions.

2 Slit the chicken breasts lengthways to make 4 pockets. Insert the SPAM filling and press the edges of the chicken together. It is a good idea to hold the edges together with wooden cocktail sticks (toothpicks) while coating and frying them. Remove the cocktail sticks before serving the chicken.

3 Mix the flour with salt and pepper and dust over the chicken breasts, then coat them with the egg and breadcrumbs.

4 Heat the butter and oil in a large frying pan and brown the chicken portions quickly on all sides. Lower the heat and cook more slowly until tender. Drain on kitchen paper and serve with mixed vegetables or a salad.

SPAM® Steaks in Port Wine

Preparation time: 10 minutes
Cooking time: 15 minutes
Serves 4

1 bunch of spring onions (scallions)
50 g/2 oz (¼ cup) butter
2 teaspoons olive oil
175 g/6 oz (2 cups) chestnut mushrooms or a mixture of mushrooms
340 g/12 oz SPAM®, cut into thick slices
4 tablespoons port
2 teaspoons Dijon mustard
carrot and courgette ribbons, to serve

1 Trim away and discard the green stalks from the spring onions and roughly chop the white part. Heat the butter and oil in a large frying pan, add the spring onions and cook until just golden in colour.

2 Add the mushrooms, cook for 3 minutes then remove from the pan with a slotted spoon on to a warmed plate. Put the SPAM steaks into the pan and heat until slightly brown on both sides. Pour the port over the SPAM and add the mustard. Return the spring onions and mushrooms to the pan and heat well.

3 Arrange the spring onions and mushrooms on a warmed serving platter and place the SPAM steaks on top. Serve with carrot and courgette ribbons.

Variation: Flavour the ingredients with a little grated root ginger instead of mustard.

Pork & Fruit Stir-fry

Preparation time: 10 minutes, plus marinating
Cooking time: 12 minutes
Serves 4–6

340 g/12 oz SPAM®
2 large oranges
1 tablespoon sunflower oil
1 mild (red) onion, finely sliced
3 carrots, cut into batons
100 g/3½ oz (2 cups) sugar snap peas (snow peas)
100 g/3½ oz (1 cup) cashew nuts
shredded spring onion (scallion), to garnish
boiled rice, to serve
Marinade:
250 g/8 oz can pineapple cubes in syrup
½ tablespoon clear honey
1 teaspoon prepared mustard
2 teaspoons grated orange rind
2 teaspoons lemon juice or vinegar
2 teaspoons soy sauce
2 teaspoons snipped chives
salt and pepper

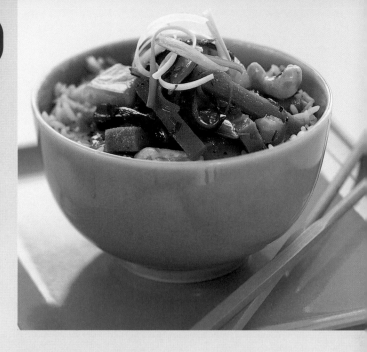

1   To make the marinade, drain the syrup from the pineapple and measure out 5 tablespoons. Pour the measured syrup into a dish and add the rest of the marinade ingredients.

2   Cut the SPAM into 1 cm/½ inch slices and then into strips. Place the strips in the marinade and leave for 20 minutes.

3   Cut the peel and pith from the oranges, then cut out the segments – free from skin and pips.

4   Heat the oil in a wok or frying pan. Add the onion and cook for 2 minutes, then add the carrots and stir-fry for 5 minutes. Put in the sugar snap peas and stir for 1 minute then add the SPAM plus the marinade, the pineapple, oranges and cashews. Heat thoroughly then garnish with spring onions and serve with rice.

Hawaiian Pork

If you are using canned pineapple rings, use the juice as part of the cooking liquid for the rice.

Preparation time: 20 minutes
Cooking time: 20 minutes
Serves 4–6

1 tablespoon groundnut or sunflower oil
2 onions, chopped
1 green (bell) pepper, cored, deseeded and diced
1 red (bell) pepper, cored, deseeded and diced
4 celery sticks, chopped
3 canned water chestnuts, sliced
1 tablespoon cornflour (cornstarch)
300 ml/½ pint (1¼ cups) chicken stock
1 tablespoon light soy sauce
340 g/12 oz SPAM®, cut into strips about 5 cm/2 inches long and
  1.5 cm/½ inch thick
5 fresh or canned pineapple rings, each cut into 4 portions
100 g/3½ oz (scant 2 cups) bean sprouts
salt and pepper
finely sliced lemon rind, to garnish
boiled rice, to serve

1 Heat the oil in a wok or large frying pan, add the onions and cook for 5 minutes then put in the peppers, celery and water chestnuts and continue stir-frying for a further 5 minutes.

2 Blend the cornflour with the stock and soy sauce. Add to the pan and stir over the heat until slightly thickened.

3 Put in the SPAM and pineapple and stir-fry for 5 minutes. Finally add the bean sprouts and salt and pepper and heat for just 1–2 minutes. Garnish with finely sliced lemon rind and serve with boiled rice.

54

SPAM® Goulash

This is a satisfying stew, based on a classic Hungarian dish. Brands of paprika vary in strength, so add the paprika gradually so you can assess the taste.

Preparation time: 25 minutes
Cooking time: 30 minutes
Serves 4

2 tablespoons olive oil

3 onions, thinly sliced

2 garlic cloves, finely chopped

1 tablespoon paprika, or to taste

400 g/13 oz (2 cups) canned chopped plum tomatoes

150 ml/¼ pint (⅔ cup) water

500 g/1 lb potatoes, cut into 2.5 cm/1 inch slices

340 g/12 oz SPAM®, cut into 4 cm/1½ inch dice

salt and pepper

bread, to serve

To garnish:

yogurt

flat leaf parsley sprigs

1 Heat the oil in a large saucepan, add the onions and cook steadily for 5 minutes. Add the garlic and paprika and stir over the heat for 2 minutes. Paprika burns easily, so stirring is important.

2 Add the tomatoes and water, stir, then bring to the boil. Add a little salt and pepper and the potatoes. Cover the pan and cook steadily for 10–12 minutes, or until the potatoes are nearly tender.

3 Add the SPAM and cook for a further 5 minutes. Taste and adjust the seasoning if necessary then garnish with yogurt and parsley and serve with bread.

SPAM® Fact

The Hawaiians are keener on SPAM® than any other nation.

Easy Cooking

There are many popular convenience foods on the market – SPAM˚ being a good example. When time is precious, buy frozen vegetables – there is no preparation and the vitamins are retained. Small bags of mixed salad ingredients are a good buy; you get a variety and save wastage. Make sure your diet includes enough protein and a good proportion of fruit and vegetables.

Meaty Chowder: The term 'chowder' has come to mean a soup so full of ingredients that it makes a main dish. Add diced vegetables to your favourite soup; cook until the vegetables are nearly tender then add diced SPAM and heat thoroughly.
• Serve the chowder topped with chopped herbs. These can be bought chopped and frozen; just take out the amount required.
• If you do not want to prepare fresh garlic look for available alternatives, including garlic salt.

Pasta Dishes
• Try the recipe for **Neapolitan SPAM˚ & Penne** on page 48.
• **Eastern Noodles:** Cook and drain the required quantity of pasta and return it to the pan. Add a little peanut butter, whisked eggs and finely chopped SPAM and stir over the heat until the eggs are set. Top with peanuts (make sure no one is allergic to them) and desiccated coconut.
• For a quick **Italian pasta dish**, heat cooked pasta with chopped fresh or canned tomatoes or pesto sauce, add frozen peas and diced SPAM and heat well.

Rice Dishes
The rice dishes on page 49 are simple to make and can be varied according to your ingredients.

Pasta and Rice Salads
Cooked pasta and rice are excellent as the basis for salads. Remember these are perishable foods when cooked, so store them only for a limited time in the refrigerator, or freeze them.

If you like pastry but find it troublesome to make buy **filo pastry**. Use oil for brushing the sheets to save melting butter. For a dish to impress your friends make the SPAM Wellington recipe, below.
SPAM˚ Wellington: Prepare several layers of filo pastry, according to packet instructions. Spread the centre with finely chopped mushrooms blended with a little oil and chopped parsley. Place 340 g/12 oz SPAM in the middle of the mushroom-coated pastry. Fold this around the meat to make a neat parcel and seal firmly. Place on a baking sheet. Make a slit on top, brush with a little more oil and bake for 30–35 minutes in a preheated oven, 200°C/400°F/Gas Mark 6, reducing the heat slightly after 20 minutes. Serve hot.

SPAM® Fan Clubs

Where is the SPAM fan club?

Bury House
125–126 Cromwell Rd
London SW7 4ET

We are used to hearing about fan clubs, but a fan club for a luncheon meat is certainly unexpected. Nevertheless there are flourishing Official SPAM Fan Clubs in both the USA and in Britain.

How did this happen?

The answer for the USA is provided by Hormel Foods in these words: 'We didn't come up with the idea of a SPAM fan club. People like you did. You sent us photos. You wrote touching stories. You came up with tasty recipes. And more. Why the only thing left for us to do was organize a fan club.'

People joining the Club in America pay a $15 annual fee and in return they get a member's shirt, a special certificate plus a club card and the quarterly newsletter, known as **A Slice of Spam**.

That is certainly not the end of the story, for members are encouraged to make their voices heard by sending in regular contributions about their experiences, special SPAM recipes and problems to be solved. There are regular events held in the birthplace of SPAM – Austin, Minnesota – and elsewhere. In Anchorage, Alaska, there is a Night Club with a revue, based on Alaskan culture. This includes SPAM mentions and members of the Fan Club enjoy a SPAM menu.

Over the years a special range of merchandise has become available including a **Party Pack**, which includes all the things you will need for a successful SPAM party. There are items of personal wear and pieces of kitchen and sporting equipment as well.

The British SPAM Fan Club was formed fairly recently and it is proving a great success. Membership grows and the fans are enthusiastic about the various activities. There is no charge for joining the British SPAM Fan Club. Several special items, such as T-shirts, ties and earrings, are available for sale to club members.

The regular newsletter is called **The SPAM™tastic Times**. This contains current news items, new recipes based upon SPAM and details of competitions. Recently a lucky fan, who was acclaimed the **SPAMite of the Year**, won a holiday in Hawaii. Members are invited to contribute news and any other items. From one issue of the newsletter I quote a few lines from a poem sent in recently.

SPAM is fab, SPAM is cool
SPAM's enough to make you drool.
Good on toast, good on bread
Brill on earrings that hang from your head,
I've become accustomed to the taste of SPAM.

The History of Fritters

Throughout the ages some form of fritters have been a feature of menus in many parts of the world so it is possible that with the ever-increasing popularity of SPAM, the recipe on page 59 is now made around the globe.

In his book *The Pantropheon*, a history of food in ancient times, published in 1853, Alexis Soyer describes fritters as a delicacy made in Greek and Roman times. These were prepared with flour, kneaded with wine, seasoned with pepper and then worked up with milk and finally with a little fat or oil. Some cooks worked sesame flour with honey and oil and then fried the mixture.

In the 19th century the accomplished cookery writer Eliza Acton gave a recipe for making what she calls Plain Common Fritters, in which a generous proportion of eggs were mixed with flour and milk and fried in hot lard. There is no suggestion in her book that the mixture was used to coat foods. An even better known writer of the same century, Mrs Beeton, gives recipes for a large selection of sweet and savoury fritters. She uses various kinds of batter to coat fruit, fish and meat and the fritters are fried in fat. Today, of course, we use oil for frying in most cases.

One of the greatest chefs of all time, Escoffier, put recipes for various fritter batters in his book *A Guide to Modern Cookery*, published in 1907. On the whole, he favoured water or beer, rather than milk, as the liquid in the coating batter.

When one comes to the 1940s, there are many references to **SPAM® Fritters**. These were made by cooks in the Armed Forces, in private homes but above all else in schools. Ask anyone who was a British schoolchild during the years of rationing (1940–1954) about their favourite school main dish and I have no doubt that in most instances you will be told that it was **SPAM® Fritters**. The basic recipe on page 59 is a good example of the one that would have been made at that time, except that today we can use fresh eggs and fresh milk, rather than the dried varieties. We can also substitute beer for milk – quite a difficult thing to do in the 1940s when beer, although not rationed, was not in plentiful supply. Any on sale was considered essential for drinking but not for cooking.

SPAM
CHOPPED PORK AND HAM

SPAM® Fritters

Preparation time: 10 minutes
Cooking time: 3–6 minutes per batch
Serves 4

340 g/12 oz SPAM®
oil, for frying or deep-frying
spring onion (scallion) mash, to serve
chopped herbs, to garnish
Batter:
125 g/4 oz (1 cup) plain (all-purpose) flour
pinch of salt
1 large egg
125 ml/4 fl oz (½ cup) milk, or milk and water,
    or water or beer

1 Mix together all the batter ingredients in a bowl. The mixture should be thick, in the proportions given above, in order to coat the SPAM well. Cut the SPAM into 8 slices.

2 Meanwhile, heat 2–3 tablespoons oil in a frying pan or wok or heat a depth of oil in a deep-fryer to 170°C/340°F or until a cube of day-old bread turns golden in 1 minute.

3 Coat the SPAM slices once or twice with the batter then drop them into the hot oil. If shallow-frying allow 2–3 minutes on each side;

if deep-frying allow a total cooking time of 3–4 minutes, turning over the fritters as required. Drain on kitchen paper, garnish with fresh herbs and serve with spring onion mash.

Variations: Make the batter with 2 eggs and reduce the liquid by 2 tablespoons.
• For a light 'puffy' batter, use 1 teaspoon baking powder and separate the egg(s). Add the yolk(s) to the flour, then the liquid and lastly the whisked white(s), just before coating the SPAM.
• Add 1 tablespoon oil or melted butter to the batter to give extra crispness.
• Mix cooked sweetcorn and diced SPAM with chopped herbs. Add to the batter and fry in spoonfuls.

Thai SPAM® Cakes

Preparation time: 15 minutes
Cooking time: 15 minutes
Serves 4

500 g/1 lb potatoes, cooked
25 g/1 oz (2 tablespoons) butter
3 tablespoons canned coconut milk
2 teaspoons chopped basil
1 tablespoon sunflower oil
1 onion, finely chopped
2 teaspoons Thai green or red curry paste
340 g/12 oz SPAM®, finely diced
pinch of chilli powder (optional)
2 teaspoons lime juice
2–3 tablespoons flour
3 tablespoons sunflower oil
salt and pepper
To serve:
lime wedges
thinly sliced onion
lime rind

1 Mash the potatoes with the butter and coconut milk, add the basil and beat well. Heat the oil in a saucepan, add the onion and cook for 5 minutes.

2 Stir in the curry paste, heat for 1 minute then blend with the potatoes. Add the SPAM, chilli powder, if using, and lime juice and season with salt and pepper. Mix thoroughly then form into 8 round cakes. Coat with the flour.

3 Heat the oil in a frying pan, add the SPAM cakes and fry until crisp and brown on both sides. Serve with lime wedges, thinly sliced onion and lime rind.

Variation: Children's SPAM® Cakes: Mix equal amounts of mashed potatoes and finely diced or mashed SPAM. Flavour with herbs or a little tomato ketchup or chutney and form into cakes. Coat them in flour then with beaten egg and dried breadcrumbs. Fry until crisp and brown.

Because SPAM is already cooked it can be heated within minutes. There are many different ways in which it can make a satisfying and interesting hot dish. Here are three suggestions. Each dish serves 4.

Grilled SPAM® and Pineapple: Place fairly thick slices of SPAM from a 340 g/12 oz can on a sheet of foil placed on the rack of a grill pan. Brush each slice with a few drops of oil or melted butter. Grill under a preheated grill (broiler) until very hot and just beginning to brown, then top each slice with a well-drained canned pineapple ring and heat for 2 minutes. Meanwhile, blend the pineapple juice or syrup with arrowroot – allowing 1 teaspoon to each 250 ml/8 fl oz (1 cup). Pour into a saucepan with 1–2 tablespoons dry sherry and stir over the heat until thickened and clear. Serve with the hot SPAM.

SPAM® in Cumberland Sauce: First make the sauce. Grate the rind from ½ lemon and cut the rind from 2 large oranges into matchstick pieces (quite easy to do with a zester or even a potato peeler). Soak the two kinds of rind in 300 ml/ ½ pint (1¼ cups) water for 5 minutes. Meanwhile, squeeze the juice from the ½ lemon and the 2 oranges. Put the citrus rind and the water into a saucepan and simmer for 10 minutes then transfer it to a frying pan. Blend 1 teaspoon arrowroot with the fruit juice and add it to the pan with 4 tablespoons redcurrant jelly,

Hot and Speedy SPAM®

1 teaspoon prepared English mustard, a good pinch of ground ginger and 2 tablespoons port. Stir over the heat until slightly thickened. Slice 340 g/12 oz SPAM fairly thinly, add to the pan and poach gently until piping hot. This dish is delicious with young carrots and rice or new potatoes.

SPAM® in Creamy Mustard Sauce: Blend 2–3 teaspoons mustard powder with 25 g/1 oz (¼ cup) flour. Heat 25 g/1 oz (2 tablespoons) butter in a large saucepan, stir in the flour then add 300 ml/½ pint (1¼ cups) milk and 4 tablespoons single (light) cream. Bring slowly to the boil, stir well and cook until thickened. Slice 340 g/12 oz SPAM, add to the sauce and heat thoroughly. Garnish with parsley, a chopped hard-boiled egg and crisp croûtons (see page 28).
Variation: A few sliced or whole mushrooms can be cooked and added to the mustard sauce with the SPAM.

SPAM® in the Future

SPAM on the WEB!

At the beginning of the 21st century SPAM is a firm favourite throughout much of the world. In the USA its parent company Hormel Foods Corporation continue to produce vast quantities of this canned luncheon meat, and the enthusiasm for the SPAM Fan Club in that country continues to grow; it is described in more detail on page 57. In Britain SPAM is produced under licence by Tulip International of Denmark and distributed by that company, which is based in Norfolk, England. This firm is noted for their high quality products. The British SPAM Fan Club flourishes: there is more about it on page 57.

Naturally SPAM figures on the Hormel Website and the following information is taken from there.

'This is the one and only official SPAM Website, brought to you by the makers of SPAM Luncheon Meat. All of the others have been created by somebody else. We are not associated with those other websites and are not responsible for their content. As a Company, we are opposed to content that is obscene, vulgar or otherwise not "family friendly". We support positive family values and you can count on us for 'safe surfing' by your children.'

In America Hormel Foods Corporation announce plans for a new SPAM Museum and Visitor Centre in downtown Austin.

SPAM ™ JAM

1891. A state-of-the-art auditorium, accommodating 100 people, is designed to allow for corporate video presentations to visiting tour bus groups who will also have the option of enjoying specially prepared **SPAMBURGER** hamburgers or other **SPAM** luncheon meat specialities in an adjacent diner area.'

It is interesting to learn that the words 'spam' or 'spamming' refer to the action of sending unsolicited commercial e-mail (UCE). The official reaction from Hormel is as follows:

'We do not object to use of this slang term to describe **UCE**, although we do object to the use of our product image in association with that term. Also, if the term is to be sed, it should be used in all lower-case letters to distinguish it from our trademark **SPAM**, which should be used with all uppercase letters.'

As we look back over the sixty years since the advent of SPAM and then at its great success we must salute the observation made by George A. Hormel when he first started the company in 1891.

Innovate — don't imitate.

'The building's interior will be remodeled to accommodate a new **SPAM** and Hormel Foods museum and visitor's center, to be located on the north side, as well as office space for company employees and departments. The planned 16,550 square foot museum and visitors' center replaces the current and much smaller **SPAM** and Hormel Foods museum at OakPark Mall which has only 1,000 square feet and consists of just 500 artifacts and historical photographs.

'The greatly expanded museum area will include interactive video screens and kiosks as well as a planned history walk with exhibits and displays which follow the company's progression from its founding in

SPAM

Index

PICTURE ACKNOWLEDGEMENTS
Front Cover, Back Cover centre, Front Flap
Hormel Foods Corporation
Back Cover top left Hormel Foods
Corporation/ The British Library
Newspaper Library
Back Cover top right Rex Features
Back Cover bottom left Octopus
Publishing Group/ Sean Myers
Back Flap courtesy of the author

SPECIAL PHOTOGRAPHY
Octopus Publishing Group Ltd./ Anja
Koch 4 left, 4 right, 4 top, 5 left, 5
right, 5 Centre, 9, 27, 46/ Sean Myers
21, 22, 23, 25, 28, 29, 31, 38, 39, 40, 43,
45, 48, 50, 51, 52, 53, 54, 55, 59, 60

Hormel Foods Corporation title, 6, 7
right, 8 left, 8 bottom left, 8–9, 11 top,
11 bottom, 12 right, 12 left, 15 top, 15
bottom, 17, 26, 33, 47, 62 bottom left,
62 top right, 63
Hulton Getty Picture Collection 7 left,
16 top
Ministry of Food: Food Facts
(11.05.42)/ Imperial War Museum
Department of Printed Books 17 top
right
Popperfoto16 bottom
Python (Monty) Pictures Ltd. 34, 35
Rex Features 14